TREBLE

TREBLE

EVELYN LAU

POLESTAR
An Imprint of Raincoast Books

Raincoast Books acknowledges the ongoing financial support of the Government of Canada through The Canada Council for the Arts and the Book Publishing Industry Development Program (BPIDP); and the Government of British Columbia through the BC Arts Council.

Editor: Lynn Henry
Interior design: Teresa Bubela

LIBRARY AND ARCHIVES CANADA CATALOGUING IN PUBLICATION

Lau, Evelyn, 1971-
          Treble / Evelyn Lau.

Poems.
ISBN 1-55192-789-6
          1. Title.
PS8573.A7815T74 2005   C811 .54   C2004-906983-7

LIBRARY OF CONGRESS CONTROL NUMBER: 2005901197

Raincoast Books
9050 Shaughnessy Street
Vancouver, British Columbia
Canada, V6P 6E5
www.raincoast.com

At Raincoast Books we are committed to protecting the environment and to the responsible use of natural resources. We are acting on this commitment by working with suppliers and printers to phase out our use of paper produced from ancient forests. This book is one step towards that goal. It is printed on 100% ancient-forest-free paper (40% post-consumer recycled), processed chlorine- and acid-free, and supplied by New Leaf paper. It is printed with vegetable-based inks. For further information, visit our website at www.raincoast.com. We are working with Markets Initiative (www.oldgrowthfree.com) on this project.

Printed in Canada by Houghton Boston
10 9 8 7 6 5 4 3 2 1

For John

CONTENTS

PART ONE

THE RED WOMAN

THE RED WOMAN

Some nights her body lay clasped
between ours in bed,
when I trembled it was but an echo
of her trembling,
and I could not reach you
could not reach round the white risen dough
of her flesh, her maculate skin,
always her hair. How you loved her hair,
the red sea crowning her,
the alive red girl
with eyes blue as faded denim.
You might have conjured her in story or verse,
she might have stepped out of those pages
but for the sulk in her face,
for the wilting gaze, the cleaving smile
(though even that could be sexy).

She was a lifetime commitment from the start.
She stepped out of one your books
into your arms, and whispered, *Save me.*
I know that melting. The woman scarred,
the angel flying too close to the ground.
In her past, a cruel and absent father
then husband, meals from the Food Bank,

holes in her jeans —— that was what
turned you on. Under your care
her hair grew like a princess's,
lavish as fed grass,
it carpeted the floor of the apartment,
flowed out the door and into the street,
a blood river of red
we walked upon hand in hand
in the winking light of evening,
returning from a matinee or supper
at the neighbourhood cafe.

It was the year of redheads. Red was in.
Angie Everhart pouted from the pages of *Elle*,
orange-red hair down to her breasts.
Redheads swung through the pages
of that year's fiction list,
having more fun than anyone.
I bought red dresses, red T-shirts,
red satin blouses, but it wasn't the same.
They licked ceilingward in my black closet
and set off the sprinkler system
with their closeted heat.
I dreamt of the red woman:

in a flying dream, I swooped down upon her,

butterfly scissors in hand,

I gathered up the harvest of her red hair

swarming through my fingers,

I cut and cut

but it grew back threefold,

more monstrous still.

In another dream you roared towards me

in a race-car, come to claim me with diamonds,

but the passenger door was painted

with her face, red hair snaking out;

she was the figurehead on the battleship,

the iron maiden, the tattoo.

Once I dreamt of making love to her

so I could come close to you

but she was slippery, she wore a dress

of fish scales, azure and aquamarine,

she wriggled out of my arms and lolled

on the floor, flipping out of reach.

In reality she was overweight

and ponderous, scarred more by acne

than a heroine's tragic past,

but her hair sprang forth
rust-red, red as a party dress,
a surging flame, a burning passion.
If she were in prison, her hair
would grow out through the bars, shape itself
into a key, and unlock the locked door.
You kept photographs of her
posed in parking lots, doorways, alleys —
her hair the one alive thing in a landscape
bled of colour. Her hair a plant,
a magician's cape,
a dagger in your heart.
You could make a silky skin of it,
a valentine, a chenille blanket, a lash, a whip.
Imagine yourself tied to a bed
roped by her red hair.

Her hair sent out flares
that landed all around you, burning.
You didn't stand a chance.
You surrendered hot, weak and coughing,
on your knees and cowed.
She smelled of cherry licorice
and the forbidden roses in a neighbour's garden.
Your eyes reflected red.

But there was a trick to keeping you.
I learned it, as the hopeful bride
learns from *Joy of Cooking*.
The trick was to need you more,
to fly so close to the ground it became
like crawling.

SMALL

I lay in your arms like a doll.
I was limp as a rag,
my limbs like noodles,
my hair a dandelion parachute,
my heart a cinnamon heart
flicked by your tongue.
I was so small.
I watched you with tiny button eyes,
fixed you in my hollow sight.

For a while you loved me.
I was cream poured out of the pitcher,
on your tongue I was tapioca pudding,
lemon custard, strawberry shortcake.
I was shaped like a pink pout.
I purred. I needed no nourishment
but your embrace. My self was tiny
as a grain of sugar.
You could have put me on your tongue,
swallowed me whole.

You tried to keep me.
You held my hand at the crosswalk,
kissed my cuts and scrapes,

fed me strained squash and applesauce

from glass Heinz jars and told me

I was cuter than the Heinz baby.

But it was no use.

I was empty inside,

I failed to thrive.

You were all I hungered for,

wept for til you were sick of my weeping,

til your body drew back like a bow.

I've given you everything, you said,

what more do you want!

I was not your daughter, after all.

Panic tumbled in you,

anger swarmed your throat like bees.

I was *too* little. Like a bean.

You could squish me flat with your thumb,

with a word or a look.

Soon I grew so small

I became invisible to you.

You looked for me everywhere

but I wasn't playing hide-and-seek.

I was lost.

"RAGTIME" OPENING AT FORD THEATRE, MAY 10, 1998

A year later, I see you
in the theatre lobby at intermission,
your aged face two-faced in the segmented mirror
above the twin staircases. I feel enough
to turn away. Too late.
You've fixed me in your gaze,
and the belling in my chest,
the emptied lungs, the seized throat,
might not be hammering hatred
but the breathlessness of first love.

Then, as if in a movie version
of the moment when lust is sparked,
the crowd dissolves
and we are standing in the stripped room
lovers inhabit, our bodies burning
in a single flare of fury,
and I see: even hatred binds
and the union is unbroken.

How have we arrived here,
your face as unknowable to me
as a thief's surprised at the foot of the bed

after he steals in from the window

and I wake from a nightmare

to find a stranger in the room?

EXAMINATION FOR DISCOVERY

Across the street, a curtain blows
in a high window of a hotel —
a white flag, or a sail on open sea.
Here, nothing comforts
in this cold room. Blue evidence binders
bristling with yellow tabs, the court reporter's
rapid tapping on her strange machine,
scars of light across our sere faces.

I swear to tell the truth, nothing but
the truth, as if that might break
the seal of silence, and my heart would open,
but when I say *I do*
I am thinking of the couples who take
that long and final walk down the aisle,
past the curious faces along every row,
to stand before the judge who bows his head
and grants not a marriage, but divorce.

Yet I came expecting to see a stranger,
perhaps the one you've become in my dreams,
the one who greets me first with a kiss
then a blinding blow. Here you are as familiar
as the time I saw you on the street

and walked an entire block behind you, wondering
how you stayed so shut inside yourself
you never turned around, or knew.

Now your words fill the air
with a storm of black stings,
and I make a small incision in my skin
to let them in. *Cruel, mean, evil*, you say,
turning to me again under the lights,
and I let you in. Around the table
our grim faces yield nothing,
as if words had come to cost a fortune,
and the first of us to gasp
in pain would lose.

THE DIVORCE HOUSE

The divorce house is dirty plates
and food spills, gum wadded
under sofas and banisters,
a zoo of toys. An envelope
on the kitchen table, its return address
reading "Attorney-at-law", its contents cramped
with the language of litigation.
This is the last task of love.
After dinner you bend over the dishes
in the sink, scrubbing hard and shouting
at me while I gather your daughter's milky bowls,
fold my guest towels into exact squares,
pity your ex-wife.

Saturday we drive to the marina.
On the boat we are children
adrift in a toy vessel, and the bathtub sea
never hints at hypothermia,
or the sea-monsters housed
in its 600-foot depths.
The day is salt sun, sea wind.

Years ago I dreamed
I was in love with you, and woke
stretching like a cat
in a square of sun.

Now the wheel in my hands
is a puzzle I am too slow to solve,
so that suddenly the smear of land
dissolves in a slipping second,
and bottles crash and roll
below as we tip and veer.
You whirl round in a rage,
words flying like blades,
and I stand in a corner of the boat,
too ashamed to sit. I won't
dream that dream again.

The divorce house waits for us,
your heavy footfall on the hard floor,
the slam of the bedroom door.
The cat licks my hand,

begs for love, then flees

at my first mean glance.

In the green parlour I dream

my lawyer arrives for dinner,

but instead of a bottle of wine

or a spray of roses he holds out

his only offering:

documents for my signature.

Together we empty the fridge,

the cupboards, weeping

as we prepare this final feast.

DRUNK DRIVING

We were driving the wrong way
down a one-way street
when the police car cruised past,
swerved sharply round.
The officer gave an angry shout
and the night became a circus
of swimming lights and sirens,
blue-red, disco-bright.
You got out of the car, stood small
and calm in his brute vision,
lies like tiny bells tinkling
from your throat.
The sight of your smooth thighs
in their short-shorts stopped him
so that I heard his halting breath,
and knew that if beauty
is believed to equal goodness,
as the studies show, then
he would let you go.

We drove away drunk
to another bar, we who as girls
had lain in pink beds, reading
Gone With the Wind and torn Harlequins,

picturing ourselves princesses
who would grow up to live in castles
with princes who rode white horses
and never left.
When I closed my eyes the world
was dark and drained, and turned
slowly in a lightless merry-go-round.
That night I dreamt I was at the doctor's,
he and I separated by a row of mirrors
reflecting us back to ourselves,
and though I tried to shout my misery
it merely bounced back to me —
my words flew round the room like birds
and broke against the walls.
Outside the closed windows
beautiful blondes in bikinis
played volleyball, surfed and swam
under a faraway California sun.

THE KISS

Cupid was on the prowl. He raised his bow
and aimed his arrow at our table
in a corner of the restaurant, he was a grown man
with the face of a child, pudgy winged body
wrapped in a white garment
more like a toga than the garb of a god.
The foil tip pierced my shoulder
and that was our destiny. A group of girls
leaned forward to watch, faces tilted
and eager, eyes shining with gin,
as if you were the one I sought,
the one lost to hubris long ago. *Just one kiss,*
Cupid pleaded, *even on the cheek is okay.*
Everyone was watching and waiting.
It was a harder job than he'd been led to believe,
this business of stitching together what was severed,
what never was. The girls at the next table
called out encouragement like a back-up band
of angels, and I could not believe the depth
of their desire for our happiness,
for us to have found each other,
for this to be true. You leaned over
and kissed me, to put us out of our misery,

and the applause rose in the room

along with the winged thing

that flew out of my heart like one of the evils

out of Pandora's Box when it was opened.

THE SINKING HOUSES

It was only a landscape painting,
tucked away in the back of the gallery —
a green peninsula scattered with houses,
a boat drifting in blue water.
But there were no boundaries
anywhere in this reflected world,
no gardens or fences or shielding trees
between the houses that were sinking
as if into quicksand, their tiny doors opening
onto darkness, the people gone.
I wanted to tell you a story
about the people with no boundaries,
to see the pain on your face like a flame
that burns neighbourhoods down,
but instead I told you about the dwarf
trapped inside the littlest orange house,
condemned to live alone forever.
We walked laughing out of the gallery,
drank wine on a sun-filled patio,
barbecued steaks for dinner and played house
like grown-ups. That night you dreamt
you saved me. You, who never wanted
to save anyone, reached down
and pulled me up out of the water.

The rooftops were almost level
with the tall grass, and there was
no human sound for miles
but the pounding of the blood in your wrist
like a man running in the dark.

THE CORN MAZE

I followed you in. The path split,
doubled back, curved round,
and we circled for hours
under the flat summer sky, down green halls
and corridors, some in shadow,
some in light, where other couples
stumbled in defeat. They crashed past us
in the heat, we could see them flickering
through the rows, husbands and wives,
teenagers in lust, searching for the prize
promised us in the storybooks —
the knight in armour, the girl's hair
a ladder of light.

The brochure said only the pure of heart
would find the centre of the maze,
the pale space around which this green architecture
had been planted, so we had to cheat
to find our way in, squeeze through the stalks
to the clearing in the corn forest.
The treasure chest was empty, no gold pieces
or costume jewels, yet we laughed
when other faces flashed past

and missed the hidden turn, the door
into the heart. We had arrived
in that promised place, and for a moment
this might have been the core of our world,
a place of oxygen and sunlight,
not the centre of the dark labyrinth
where the monster stretched in his sleep.

I LOVE YOU

Fifty times a day you said it.
Anyone else would have died of boredom,
but for me it was the hook that slid under skin,
buried itself in bone.
Each time I tried to leave,
the line stretched taut
so I stumbled in the open doorway.
You said it in your sleep
and woke me from dreaming about you,
your father-face gazing down
upon my child-face.
You wrote it on my back
with a finger dipped in acid,
substituting the words
with a heart and a horseshoe.
You left love notes in every room,
so many stacked around me I gasped
for breath like an asthmatic.
I'd waited my whole life for you,
a man with mirrors instead of eyes,
and arms like lifelines for the drowning.
But your love couldn't be traded for milk or eggs.
I couldn't weigh its worth,
calculate its market value.

I couldn't spend it in the stores,

or build a big house with it in a good neighborhood.

No, not even a small house.

In the end it was too much, yet not enough —

it was beyond measure, like the soul,

so light that when the body gives it up

it vanishes like it never was.

A PHOTOGRAPH OF US

That was all you wanted.
At parties, during the holidays,
some friend's or relative's camera
would find us, our faces frozen
above a turkey, pile of presents,
smash of glasses. But we never saw
the evidence afterwards.
We became a footnote in someone's album,
pasted among undated photos,
or discarded because the host looked fat
or foolish between us.
I remember our tight snuggle
to fit inside the frame,
your smile dreamy as a drowned man's,
my neck locked in your loving chokehold
as if otherwise I might slip to the floor
like a shadow without a self.
It wasn't as if we didn't exist.
But how could you be happy
with a studio portrait, the bland blue background
and our nothing smiles?
Finally you found what you wanted
in a gallery, a mirror image
more true than our own.

This was the photograph of us:
two dolls lying face to face,
tossed on broken bedsprings
in an abandoned house.
A sheet tucked to our chins,
dirt on the floor and sunlight
struggling through the grimed window.
Our parents were gone and the house
was in ruins, but anyone could see we had each other.

PART TWO

TRAVELLING NOWHERE

TRAVELLING NOWHERE

By the side of the highway
in Montana all is vast and stone-silent.
The horizon stretches beyond my peripheral vision,
further than imagination,
and if this was all I'd seen of the world,
all I'd known of love,
I'd swear this was all there was.
The song of crickets in grazed grass,
the convex of oxygenated sky,
the fields beyond the snow fences
and the abandoned farmhouses with sky inside them.
The land that stands all around.
And not a glance from the man
in the eighteen-wheeler passing, going forever
in the direction opposite mine.

∾

By day we trace the highways past prairie
and red rock, the red cliffs of Wyoming,
red road, red earth, and when you reach
for me you are still reaching
for the red-haired woman that came before me.

Nothing here is new,
not the clawed rock of the Devil's Tower,
the largest Wall Drug in the world,
Little America or the sign advertising
"Motel and Gun Shop". I am sitting
in the wife's seat and when you reach for me
you reach into your past —
each path we take is eroded with memory.
And the rage we stoke in each other
crackles into flame.

❧

At night we sit in dusty motel rooms
gazing at the defective television,
shouting silently our litany of loss
among the baseball scores, Jeopardy clues,
scuttled talk-show lives.
This is the zero of love as it is.
Later your breath snags upon a snore
as you slip beneath the surface
of the depthless lake of sleep.
I lie awake weeping with allergies
til the popcorn ceiling blurs to cloud cover.

In the morning you stretch, yawn,

open one eye to the mirror above the washbasin.

Rainwater leaks into the sink as you shave.

In the story of "Turandot"

a slave girl followed her prince

and died for him, all because one summer day

a long time ago, he smiled at her.

That was opera. Perhaps love

is instead this wearing down,

this warm body in the same room yet far away.

Tonight the windows of the motel

go blind with lightning.

Thunder follows fast, and rain

soaking the brilliant countryside.

I've been dreaming

of a suburban house, the walls

and baseboards infested with sand fleas

like the ones we saw at Salt Lake.

I screamed in the lavender bathroom

as they rose in a haze from the tiles

and swarmed over me.

You lay in the master bedroom.

You knew nothing, though the house around us

crumbled as you slept.

RODEO DRIVE

we drove towards LA from the desert
down Highway 10, Johnny Cash on the tape deck
keeping a close watch on that heart of his
on Rodeo Drive a black beggar
with the manners of a gentleman
tipped his hat to you
and for the first time you gave
until your pockets were empty

at the Gucci store the sales staff looked to our shoes
for clues as to the state of our hearts
to divine our intentions
or were we just flirting with their affections
you touched a sweater folded on a glass shelf
searching for the price hidden away
in its bitter bice heart
the buried heart with its figures and calculations
the price you'd have to pay
it was soft as a shivering animal
a cloud of gunmetal shavings
a thousand dollars worth of blue
but what we wanted was more
a price so perfect it could not be paid
and so we went from store to store

upstairs at Tiffany's we came upon the glass case

of engagement rings as upon a treasure chest

sunk in sand or sea

diamonds as real as glass

your face grew confused with their constellations

so bright I could not look at you

diamonds where your eyes were

diamonds in each nostril, and one perfect

diamond nestled winking in the cleft of your chin

desire and fear played their swift fingers down my body

until I was cut in half

a cluster of panic gathered in my stomach

greed like a gold apple caught in my throat

and Johnny Cash singing

I keep my eyes wide open all the time

I thought of the divorce papers you would soon sign

the booklet where John Que Public lived on Divorce Lane

and Joan Que Public lived on Alimony Road

and how one night in a bar

over brandy balloons and shucked oysters

my friend said *Do you know how many divorced men*

it takes to screw in a light bulb?

How many? I asked

It doesn't matter, he's not going to get the house anyway
and when I told you that one you laughed
weakly as though we were having some other conversation
beneath the one we were having

later in Santa Monica at the Shangri-La Hotel
the ocean outside buried in fog
a poster in our room showed "LA Over New York"
the two cities, one drowned
one with its palm trees in the air
and as we slept on the cold mattress
fog like influenza crept into our lungs
and in a dream I saw you
bending forward again over the glass case
with the look of someone about to place
his face in water for the first time

THE RAINBOW WASN'T ENOUGH

The day, miraculously, continues.
The morning I learn of your suicide,
FLARE Magazine arrives in the mail
along with the phone bill and the usual
detritus of advertisements.
Frozen orange juice for 89 cents at Safeway.

Errands to run, then a drive
across the border for dinner at the Semiahmoo Inn
where I drink a glass of wine and convey
pieces of food from plate to mouth as usual.
Life goes on. The water is black

beyond the pier and the window reflects
my corporeal self in a white sweater,
my reflection which is skin and heat,
pulse and platelets, which gestures
and thinks, *I am alive.*

What makes me alive when you
are dead? I ponder my tongue
resting in my mouth and am confused
by its existence, but life
as it is goes on: the routine

of Mastercard bills, gasoline, groceries,
the meals one must eat to sustain life.
After dinner a drive back
across the border to Shannon's Arcade
to play air hockey and I compete
til my fingers are bruised.

If I can just guard my goal,
the wide black mouth
where the air hockey puck will glide
and disappear, surely I can guard you
from your death.

The puck slams past my defence,
it slips silently into the goal
though I am vigilant, though I try my best
to keep you safe. You slide past me into
death where there are no yellow diners

to go for breakfast in mid-afternoon,
no late nights of gin and conversation,
no mornings driving past Main and Hastings
in the Rolls-Royce while the pinched faces
of passersby poke at us among the neons,

pale with envy for what they thought we had
but didn't, not knowing
the man at the wheel was talking of suicide
while I was silent, avoiding
your pain as one does an accident

on the highway up ahead.
Not knowing we were weeks away
from the sunny, blue-sky day
I would fly to Montreal
and you would sit in the garage
with the engine running.

Now I wake clawing my way out of dreams
where I search for you
and pull you to safety, but the truth is
by the time I reach the garage where you are,
it's too late. That summer day

at the yacht club when we walked to the end
of the pier, sun burst through rain,
a rainbow arced above us, and you said,
Always remember the rainbow. I was sad
over some blighted love, and barely listened,
because the rainbow wasn't enough.

"WE, AMNESIACS ALL"

(after Geoffrey Sonnabend, Obliscence: Theories of Forgetting and the Problem of Matter, *1946. Museum of Jurassic Technology, Los Angeles, California)*

If, as Sonnabend believed,

memory is an illusion

we invented to protect ourselves

from the intolerable loss of experience,

if experience is something that otherwise passes

and is lost forever,

then at what angle do you rest

in the cones and planes of my fabricated memory?

If we are amnesiacs all

then at some angle you will vanish

from my world of decaying experience.

Every night in my dreams I open doors

to houses and futures you have vacated,

every night I ask you

the meaning of the word fortitude.

But you have forgotten. These mornings

after your suicide, when I wake

in a world where time does not bend

back on itself, and no second chances are granted

after death, and all experiences are lost

once lived, I begin to learn

Sonnabend's theory of the falsity of memory.
Once the cone of obliscence
—— real as a pancreas or spleen ——
passes through the plane of experience,
all remembered experience will disappear,
become something that never was, and so too

these days of motel rooms down the coast,
redwoods ringed from Columbus's discovery of America,
all roads marked Ocean View and every morning
a Johnny Cash Sunday morning
coming down.

VARADERO — HAVANA

One evening we discovered the square
next to our hotel, its crumbling gates
guarded by pimps and prostitutes,
yet we entered fearless
as into a garden of roses in bloom.
But this was Cuba
and poverty, where the workers bent in waves of green
in the fields, while by the pool
tourists lay half in water, half in sun,
flesh greasy and plump as roasting chickens.
At night we slept in purgatory
in our adobe room, between swift ants swaying
across the tiled floor
and mosquitoes circling the sweetness
of our laid-bare bodies.

Bravely we entered the square —
hot black eyes, ghetto music, and the signals
I kept missing: the man with his hand
by his crotch, the pair of girls
at the fountain, snug as sausages
in denim vests and pants, their mouths and fingernails
sporting the only pink polish available.
Their mouths bursting with desire

for what you might give them.

Alone, I wandered into the liquor store,

and when you returned you could hardly

pull open the glass doors between us.

I just got propositioned.

That girl there, in the black slacks,

the pretty little girl ...

You were beaming, excited, as though what she wanted

was you, and it was then I knew

she would lie between us

like the crack between our single beds

pushed together, into which

we might yet fall, and lose each other.

Ours was still the limerence stage,

the early days of lovers before routine

and resentment set in, the time when some

commit suicide to grasp forever

the gasp of surprise in the mouth of the other.

We had this impulse ourselves,

though it seemed no more than a desire for sleep.

That night the sullen maids came

to stand in the doorway in their gingham costumes
and spray poisonous fumes into our room.
We stayed, wrapped together on the beds
as poison floated and fell upon our bodies,
and the colony of ants on the tiled floor
shrivelled and died,
and the mosquitoes lost their nerve,
flying lower and lazier til they spun
straight down. We lay in each other's arms,
coughing in unison.

෴

You wonder what we will remember of Havana,
if it will be the statue on the hillside,
shifty as a mirage in the striated heat-haze,
or the flies like black pepper swarming the salad
in the open-air restaurant where chickens screamed
and peacocks strutted in the courtyard,
or the coconut we bought in the market,
its shaven skull carved into the shape
of a cup, sweet interior water,
flesh white as the milk teeth of children.

If it will be what we were shown:

the snowy memorial to Jose Marti,

the museum of the captain's general,

the palace rooms red-brocaded and filled

with old Cadillacs, old carriages,

worn carpets we were not to walk on,

each lived-in room barred by lengths of red rope

as if we were at a theatre. If it will be the bar

where Hemingway stopped for daquiris,

or the scorched market tumbled with crafts —

dominoes, mariachis, wooden women both anorexic

and zaftig, Che's face on a beaded curtain,

local art a mixture of cartoon and acid nightmare.

It will not be what we were shown.

Perhaps it will be the blond prostitute

squeezed into her sky-blue minidress and languid

in her doorway, the way Cuba will forever

be the stares of men

and the propositions of hungry women.

The way our shirts stuck to our skins,

the way we ourselves were hot and hungry.

The begging women with their babies clutched

as props in their hands, waiting for us
at the rear doors of our tour bus,
retreating across the street between busloads
of tourists to sit on the sidewalk and smoke
like construction workers taking a break
after a morning's hard labour.
The cry of disgust I gave
when a leprous woman clasped her hand
to my shoulder as though to comfort me,
smiling even when I flung her hand
back into her face and shuddered and made a show
of brushing my body clean of her.

It will be the red woman on the tour bus,
a secretary from Russia, who said she was 36,
then 28, then 12, and that her birthday
was today. The men watched her
across the aisle from their wives.
Not exactly beautiful, she had more to commend her
than beauty, she was Nikita on the other side of the border,
exotic as a bird of paradise
or a bird of prey. Her mouth was small,
sly, a petal of pink gloss, and she preened herself
constantly, drawing mirror and comb from her purse,

coaxing her red hair down around her shoulders,
back in a ponytail, up in a top knot,
barricading it with pins. I watched you
watching her. The crack between our beds widened
and I fell in. Later that night
when you breathed and turned and reached
for me I turned to you,
alert to your every move, even in sleep,
and discovered it was not you but only the wind
tossing the shadow of the coconut tree beyond our balcony.

It is the red woman we will remember.

There is a red woman in every city
of the past and the future. She is the former lover
who will never relinquish her hold over you,
she is the fantasy lover
who lurks in the doorway of a street you've yet to visit,
in the maze of dreams where you circle trapped,
and she is the woman of the present
who for a moment or an afternoon fills your sight
and enthralls you like your own daughter.

Hers is the head on the third pillow
between ours in bed, she is the one who came before
and touched you in every place
and named you hers.
She photographed you sleeping,
cut your hair and clipped your fingernails,
these intimacies more difficult
to surmount than sex.

In kindergarten the redheads were teased,
made to feel ugly, freakish,
there were certain colours they couldn't wear,
sun they couldn't stand, and then
there were the freckles. Later their lovers
would count every one, later
the heroines of your novels would have red hair,
and I would search every city
for redheads and yearn for red hair
as for another girl's lashes and frocks,
as for my father's love withheld.

On the bus from Havana back to Varadero
I slept in your lap the way an infant does,
exhausted by the vision of new things,
all my senses battered, bruised,
and at each pothole I woke
to see your face above me, your face that has slid
and locked into the face of another, my father,
floating small and clear as a face
in a rearview mirror, as the diamond
in the crystal watch-face.
Then a red-haired woman walked past,
you turned away for an instant,
and when you turned back,
my safe-keeper, my looker-after,
your eyes no longer held my reflection
but another's.

DOMESTICITY, #1

One sunlit afternoon on El Paseo Drive,
we found our reflections burned into a mirror
hung in the art gallery,
the mirror on which was written:
"Fairest of Them All."
For that instant, we were so.
Our shy, struggling faces couldn't escape
its gawk, its gilt frame.
But the glass was fickle, it reflected
the faces of all who passed.

Today the avenues are washed out.
You return to rain
and the recital of the day's memorandums,
your grocery-list voice one in which
it is harder to seek out the source of love
than in rising rages and the hand
that extends in truce. Here,
according to you, is where love begins to wilt:
in the dampening of daily life
the fabric of love wears thin,
becomes an old cotton shirt,
a frayed washcloth whose absence
you would not notice enough to miss.

DOMESTICITY, #2

It was evening,
the room flooded with misery light.
Our faces pinched with the final words
we wished to say to each other,
our jaws wired shut into silence.
My hand shook so in the brown air
that the cupboard door slammed
like a fired cannon.

I could not look upon your face
folded in on itself,
an origami of anger,
when it was the same face that once
beheld me in wonder. It seemed as if
I heard again my mother's voice —
I should have married him instead of you —
from the room at the end of the hall,
and my father speechless
with his own thoughts of murder.

Now, we could not even think.
You were sunk deep in the blue chair,
blinking at television,

while in the silence a distant hum
took hold, a sound I thought only
the electric-wire buzz of bottled rage,
but it was an airplane,
flying low between the office buildings
and condominiums all around us.

Not turning to me
you stretched out your arm to point
at its size, its spanning wings,
its belly bright as a bullet.
Look, you said, *did you see that?* —
as though we were two lovers parked in the air field,
interrupted in our embraces
by the miracle of flight.

ON BOWEN

The ferry docks in the bay,
among glass houses. Six o'clock,
hour of martinis — I prepare the gin,
the cloudy olives.
We eat dinner by candlelight,
for you a painful journey
of fork from mouth to plate —
the Parkinson's has slowed some current
of command and response, so that the body
plays dumb to the mind's instructions.
Soon you begin to yawn, and rise
from the table with your strong body
to perform the festonating walk of the P.D. patient,
that sad stutter of steps. Later I find you
in the kitchen, staring at a spoon in your hand
and shouting, *Let go, let go!*
while your fingers stubbornly hold on.
What has become of the night
we stood on your balcony in the city,
threw lit sparklers over the railing
and wished for better lives?
Here ants cascade over the tiled floors,
ferrying grains of sugar back
and forth, nimble and swift.

Vancouver Public Library
Checkout Receipt

_Central Branch
Date (MM/DD/YY): 08/09/22 05:25PM
****

Treble /
Item: 31383089089836
Call No.: YA821 L366t
Due Date (MM/DD/YY): 08/30/22

Total: 1

Item(s) listed due by closing
on date shown.

For renewals, due dates, holds, fines
check your account at www.vpl.ca
or call Telemessaging at 604-257-3830

Want to check out VPL from home?
Visit our Digital Library 24/7 to get free
online access to thousands of reads,
audiobooks, films, music and more.
vpl.ca/digital | vpl.ca/digitallibrary

Please Retain This Receipt

INDIAN SUMMER, 1998

It is your seventieth birthday, a day of sun
and massing cloud. On the ferry over
the man beside me predicts,
This day will end in tears. Whose tears?
Not mine. He says his heart
has shrivelled to something small,
a walnut, or an acorn.
It is the last Sunday of this Indian summer.

The house is filled with enough flowers
for a funeral. Out in the garden
among the tents of food and champagne,
your wife has arrived on a day pass
from the psychiatric ward, hair yellow,
eyes masked in makeup, face a stony ruin.
They won't let me wash my hair
in the hospital, she cries.
The pastor lowers his eyes,
asks us to join hands in silence,
but she shakes her head savagely
and breaks the circle
of a hundred family and friends.

You stand before us, seventy years old

and mortal, while in the kitchen your wife

starts to scream, a sound so unholy

you turn to stone. You might have made the mistake

of turning to look back

at the burning city, in remorse

or fatal curiousity. No one moves

but your brother, stepping through the crowd

as the bell and the book

drop from your trembling hands.

SIXTH FLOOR MUSEUM,
TEXAS SCHOOL BOOK DEPOSITORY, DALLAS, TEXAS

You were a third-grader,
the principal on the P.A. in tears,
and later that night when you said
what's the big deal anyway
your father turned and struck you
across the face. All this was history to me,
flat pictures in a book, a story
from the dry past. A maze of photographs,
each part-second recorded in black and white —
the shots, the slumped body,
her frantic turning, the limousine speeding
down the street past bystanders and the grassy knoll.
It was not anything that could be foretold
or delayed, his face open to the crowds,
no shadow nor moment of grief
before the exposed day turned dark.
In the photographs a president
still claps in time to his children skipping,
Jackie is painting a canvas
in a bedroom of their seaside house,
the sunlight bathes their young bodies
like a vision of the future flooding through.

TREBLE

It was the one thing we both loved —
the treble clef rendered in rose marble,
a curving column sleek as a woman's shape,
heavy as a sigh,
a struck sound lingering high
in the air of the subterranean gallery.
It kept drawing us back
like it was the first thing we shared,
or the last. The woman behind the desk
asked if we agreed on everything,
if we were that kind of couple —
Some couples come in, married forty years,
they don't agree on anything —
and we made some joke and walked

far apart together into Whistler Village.
Out of the snow-filled light
the skiers slid like angels
bound by gravity; unable to take flight
they fell all day down the side of the scarred mountain.
At the bar near the bottom of the lift
the blond teenagers with their burned faces
crowded the patio, tired, ecstatic,
stepping awkwardly in their suits
and boots as if this was a strange planet

where the simplest things had to be learned
over again. It was here you said something
or didn't say enough, in a whisper
or was it a shout that brought down the avalanche —
I could not breathe for the flood
that carried me past you into solitude.
I wanted to tell you about this drowning,
to stir a space in the snow
and show a hand, but in this place no echo
or cry for help could score the air.
We were already too far past each other
in the bright and tumbling world.

THE GLASS HOUSE

That last day the doctor drew
a portrait of us on paper,
more accurate than a photograph —
two oval figures, one split
to show the lack of a fixed self,
the other whole yet unseen,
dark on the other side of the mirror.
A few strokes of his pencil, and you were gone.
Only the weekend before
we had stayed in a house with no mirrors,
where all day we watched the reflective waves,
the splintering mercury tide.
The house turned a blank window
to every direction, spaces of watery light.
Sunday over breakfast there was a thump
on the patio, a shower of feathers,
and you jumped up, wrenched the door open,
cradled the warm and dangling body
of the bird in your palm.
Maybe it's just stunned, you said,
but I could see at a glance its broken neck,
the cranberry blood bursting from its beak.
It was too late, though you didn't know yet.

That night in our dreams we returned
to the glass house at the fair,
where as children we had turned and turned
in its greeny depths, bumping into walls
where there seemed only soft air.
How we once thrilled to the thought
of being lost there all our lives,
this transparent maze filled with strangers
we could no more save than ourselves,
groping like the blind in bright daylight.

OCEAN SHORES

This is once in a lifetime, you said,
so we had to go back again in the rain
to see the whale, so serene there
in the sand we thought it was a sculpture
on the first pass, a stone or marble creature
rising like a rock on the poured mirror
of the beach. The whale was dead,
thick blubber skin split down the middle
and guts spilled onto the sand,
blue-gray masses like wave-washed stones,
purses of stinking fluid and the slur
of the omentum. You trailed a finger
along its divided tail, and into its blind eye
no more than a slit in its side.
Once in a lifetime, so we went back
three or four times, circling the whale
until we were frozen and fought
our way back to the car through the wind
and seagulls and bits of whale
carcass scattered around the tires.
You said it came only three or four times
in a lifetime, this falling in love,
if you were lucky that is, only if you were lucky,

and that night at the Lucky Dragon Restaurant
the slip of fortune in my cookie read,
Stop searching forever. Happiness
is right there in front of you.
You were in front of me, and then I knew
leaving you was something I couldn't do
only once in a lifetime, that I would be pulled back
always to this lifeless thing between us,
the tug of its exposed body and somewhere
inside the weight of its heavy heart.

PART THREE

FATAL ATTRACTION

FATAL ATTRACTION

The weekend he returns to his wife
I rent "Fatal Attraction," pausing at the parts
I know by heart. Your red hands,
the slits at your wrists
like twin smiles leaking blood.
You had no other choice.
He was unmoved by your tears,
your windmilling arms ripping his shirt,
your pink nipples and sad sulk.
I know the rapture
of being looked after, the pinwheel of pain
turning to relief. The nip of the razor,
the sweet chemical release.
Soon you will sleep in the white bed,
knees drawn up, the softness
of bandaged wrists against your cheek.
Daddy will wait outside the door.
He won't leave you alone in the dark.

I wanted you to win. To destroy
the family, smug in its silver frame.
I know your rage. It throbs in me
like lust, but it isn't lust.
It's snatching the other children's dolls,

smashing them. Now everyone is empty.
Heads and limbs littered everywhere.
The dolls who played father and mother,
and the doll babies who never had a chance.

In the original version, I'm told, you survive.
You triumph over the wife, with her bruised eyes,
her parted thighs before the mirror.
She is pale sunlight and afternoons in the park.
She is tea in china cups and soft sighs
in the drawn bath. She does not have your pluck
and murderous courage.
She pots flowers in the greenhouse,
puts the baby to bed in the nursery.
She is no bunny-boiler,
child-kidnapper, husband-stealer.

She would never stand in the bathroom,
stabbing herself in the thigh.
I know your grief.
You were not meant to drown,
to drift underwater with your marble face staring.
To die with a hole in your heart
while the wife lowers the gun

in the doorway and the audience cheers.
You were meant to win, to be rewarded
for your persistence, like we're taught.
The kingdom and the happy home.
The lawyer husband, the precocious child,
the house in the country.
You thought he would see you in the darkness
and pull you into the firelight.
You thought that was what he promised
that time he stayed, and his pity
looked to you like love.

BABY, #1

She drowses on milk-white sheets,
frail head capped in cream,
ten fingers and toes and a plummy yawn.
She is the size of your imagination, the sum
of yourself and the afternoons in the courtroom.
Her small body weighs more on the scale
of worth than the one night in the bar
when we ascended the ladder of desire,
searching for the sunlight in the glade.
When we arrived at that place,
your family was already there. They were waiting
in the green valley, by the lake and the canoe.
Your wife lifted her face towards you
and you saw the scroll of history,
the bright globe and the wheel of devotion.
That weekend you made the baby laugh
for the first time by swinging her in
and out of your arms, pretending to let go
but holding on as she knew you would.

BABY, #2

Today on the front page of the newspaper:
a baby fell from a bridge, and survived.
Doctors explain it's the anticipation of pain
that changes the outcome, that tightens the muscles
and dooms the fall. She fell in blissful ignorance,
trees rushing past in a green stream.
It was merely the end of a flying dream.
Your daughter once tumbled twelve feet
from second floor to sunken living room,
missing counters and bookshelves and tabletops
along the way. She fell out of the sky, neither feather
nor stone, while you watched wide-eyed,
startled by this unexpected parcel
dropped from the heavens, landing soft
and whole at your feet. Today she is a grown
little girl, her photographs stacked like a fortress
around you in your office, reminders of the family
and the home that cannot be burnt down.
Now I see there will be no ending
but this one, the ground rising higher
day after day as I fall.

OSGOODE HALL

We climb the scorched staircase,
embrace under the sightless gaze
of men no longer able to judge
or defend. In the red room,
the bordello room, you turn to me,
the lies of the courtroom in your eyes,
a flake of ash on your tongue.
Outside Osgoode Hall the silver city
once was farmland, and the iron gates
still shut to form a trap, a cage that closes
around common livestock to keep them away.
On the famous steps you say
you are never leaving her,
and your finger signs the contract
on the page of air between us,
traced in oxygen, struck in stone.

INFIDELITY: A LOVE POEM

I.

        once on a green and windswept street,

        you stood outlined in tuxedo and overcoat,

        hands slipped inside silk-lined pockets.

        a photographer went down on one knee before you

        and your wife beside you, her age showing on her hands,

        the veins telling as a signature on a bank note.

        she wore a watch studded with dials and numerals,

        ruby earrings that might have been a gift from you,

        sleek hair, the ends tucked under. I already knew

        how you pushed your hands through a woman's hair

        when you left your kisses upon her face,

        how you twisted that hair up through your fingers

        as if digging through dirt for treasure.

in a pale hotel room high above the bay

our shirts drew back from our shoulders,

I bent on one knee and parted my lips,

bathed in the planetary glow of television.

below our balcony, the laughter of lovers

taking their drinks on the deck, the explosion of lanterns

as they fell one by one into the bay.

flames ripped across the oily water

like stitches peeled from unhealed flesh,

yet my body continued to burn with its own heat,

and when the fire alarms sounded along the corridors
we changed our rhythm only to match the rhythm
of the running feet outside our door —

once in the opulence of the burning city
I sat on the terrace of the Bel-Air Hotel
and watched the swans sail beneath lantern-shaped blossoms
across the lake, and wiped the tears from the face of a friend
who had loved for a decade a married man.
when at last he came, shuddering
into stillness, he would call his wife's name
into his lover's shoulder, her body hateful
beneath his hands. the swans settled their beaks
beneath their wings, all evening behind us
a procession of bridesmaids passed through the restaurant
and lobby of the hotel on their way to a wedding.
they wore their hair in buns at the napes of their necks,
dresses lucent as the wings of dragonflies.
their satin slippers drifted across the marble —

      nights in her designer beachfront home,
      my friend puts her hand to her mouth, swallows
      a blue pill, sleeps beside the warm
      round shoulder of her husband.

II.

       if I could, I would erase the wife from the photograph

       taken in the green street smelling of cement

       and perfume and leaves. it's not true

       there had to be a ring revolving around your finger

       for my blood to quicken in my veins, that I needed

       to feel that ring's warm chemical when you rounded

       the corner in the restaurant and pressed your hand

       for an instant against mine —

let me say I spent an evening on both knees

in the bathroom, vomiting remorse

when at last I glimpsed your wife beside you

across the candlelit restaurant, and the fact of her

weighed as solid as my own self on a scale,

flesh and fingers and a mouth

that has shaped itself around you —

let me say she was never far from our thoughts,

that I sniffed your body for her scent as jealously

as a wife sniffs her husband's shirts

for traces of another woman, that you shook your head

and drew your body back from my caresses,

shaping your mouth around words like love and betrayal

and commitment and loss, even though by then it was late,
I had held you for long minutes in my mouth and throat,
had felt your face blindly
in dark hotel hallways while parliamentary bells rung
across the midnight square, and you had opened your shirt
and drawn my face down upon your chest
so I could be closer to the liquid pounding
of that loyal muscle, even though I had watched you at sunrise
lift your black suit from the wardrobe
and licked my lipstick from the corners of your mouth,
and felt like laughing because my fingertips
had memorized the planes of your face
and the uneasiness of your eyelids, and because
later I would push back my hair or raise my arm
to open a cupboard and suddenly be able to smell
something of you released from the pores of my own body —

let me say I lost breath
whenever someone said your name in a crowded room —

a year later, your wife still walks
through a fog of ignorance. it's true
there were times I wanted to force that knowledge
down her throat like a stranger's penis

in a deserted parking lot,

that I imagined violences done to her,

violences so cathartic I played them again and again

in my mind like a man might

a stimulating segment of his favourite porn video —

her pretty crumpled face, her body

so often comforted in your arms

III.

it seemed you were something I lost

over and over, something I tried to find

in the market stalls at midnight in the polar sun.

I ran wildly through the railway station

after someone I thought was you,

past the racks of postcards

and the tabloids in languages I would never understand,

front page photos of missing executives

and corrupt businessmen peering sullenly

beneath the European hoods of their eyelids,

out into the staggering sun in the square

where faces peered from the anemic sky

and bodies tilted like old churches and opera houses,
down to the waterfront market

and there I spent whatever hours left in my journey
wandering among the furs skewered on metal hooks,
the vegetable bins where carrots bristled
and the heads of young leeks bulbed.
I was hoping for a glimpse of you
buying a coffee from two teenagers at the end of the dock,
fingering a silver necklace in a velvet case,
collecting cherries like a wife's rubies
in your palm —

twelve months I lived under obsession's imprisoning
unchanging sky. when I escaped across the defended border
the barrier clattered across the road behind me,
the guards lifted their caps and went to sleep
inside the borderhouse. I ran past lakes where wild roses grew,
mourning the fading of the bruise you kneaded
upon my breast. when I reached the city
the sun was setting behind the forever dying statues
of soldiers on the rooftop of the great palace,
and I saw by the bloodstain of sunset the ruined streets,
the faces of the people bladed from hunger.

thinking to escape, I plummeted underground to the Metro,
yet every face that rose to meet the city,
the empty kiosks and storm of sand and litter
that blew outside the station, was slashed on both cheeks
by your cheekbones, and when I opened the windows
of my tourist's hotel room, I was blinded by the sun's rays
striking the blue bay, setting it
on fire —

       the guards laughed to see me again
       so soon

IV.

       nights at home I lie curled
       sideways on my white bed, touching the gelatin buttons
       of the phone like the features of a lover's face,
       humming to myself the music of your wife's voice —

I came to sympathize with the grown men stalking little girls
who appeared on talk shows in the afternoon
wearing ribbons and angelic dresses, who received the audience's tears
like benedictions. sometimes the stalker
would step on stage and mumble words
his psychiatrist had said to him —

lack of mother-love, a lonely childhood on the playground,
perhaps some uncle's hand or penis where it did not belong,
and an adulthood deprived of normal relationships
with women. he would lift his eyes shyly at the camera
and say in his stupid, thick-tongued, honest way:

> *when I first looked into that little girl's eyes,*
> *my knees shook, I couldn't breathe*

> *I was in love*, the stalker said, while the audience
> hissed in hatred and dismay

V.

around us the city was burning, along the boulevard
men wheeled TV sets away from exploded windows,
families carried furniture bristling with price tags
into moving vans, teenagers leapt out of cars
with cracked headlights, yet in the hotel
the swans were white as toothpaste and content.

> my girlfriend writes me letters from the blazing hotel.
> *yesterday was his birthday*, she writes. *all month*
> *I have not been able to eat without crying, and I have lost*
> *weight. I look like a young girl again.*

days I lie in my apartment burning with fever,
nights I pull the phone plug from the wall
and lift the receiver and dial your wife's number
again and again until I sleep in the forgiving white bed.
at last I rent a room
in the hotel by the bay. all day
I sit before the entertainment
and news of the world on television, and feel
your hand inside my opened shirt, and at night
I sit by the window and watch the bodies on the beach,
smell the singed flesh, oil of coconuts.
often I see you walking
with your wife along the shore, your fingers woven through hers
as tightly as they were woven through mine
on the wooden arm of this chair, here in this room.

       once there was a woman who stood in the green street
       wearing an evening dress, while in the distance
       the sound of sirens started down the hill.
       she held her hand on your stomach,
       perhaps feeling your familiar warmth and pulse,
       perhaps as intoxicated by your scent
       as the metallic smell of night and parties to attend.
       she started to smile —

sometime in the middle of the night

you appear on my balcony, dressed in white.

there is so much moonlight and your hair is blowing.

below you the bay is cold and black and smells

of gasoline. I lie on the floor and wait,

bathed in television's eternal twilight,

for the band around your finger to spin

a golden arc into the bay,

for the night to end, the fever

to break

VANCOUVER PUBLIC LIBRARY OPENING GALA
MAY 24, 1995

I live in the house where I did not say
I love you. Every night now I repeat it
as prayer, penance, incantation. I sit
in the black armchair to summon the memory of you.
The green couch. The burnt-orange floor. This wall
where the streetlight shines at 3 A.M. ...

Parties remind me of you. Tonight a man
said your name, and the room swam with grief.
He smelled of Pierre Cardin. I leaned
into the staple of his elbow, to feel the flesh
and bone of the person who knew you, who once
shook your hand, shook your wife's hand.
Around us men and women tumbled
like chips at the bottom of a kaleidoscope.
Gowns like fish scales, tuxes like funerals.
Again, I whisper, *say it again. Love* ...

but nothing more happens, though there are
performers on stilts, Shakespearean actors in velvet,
red vodka, quail pierced by bone, though
we slide swizzle sticks into our purses for souvenirs,
laugh subversively. Though we meet and greet,
walk and talk. Though a man I once saw on his knees,

weeping, his back candy-cane striped,

his face a pomegranate of lust,

is here tonight, splendid in his suit,

chin cocked, glass raised, wife stalwart by his side.

Say it again, I yell, *love* — but the diva

opens her throat, and no one hears.

FIREWORKS

We watch the fireworks from your balcony,
your husband with a circle of gold
on a tarnished chain round his neck,
your silk-shirted lover holding hands
with his wife, her face a dark jewel
turning in the lit-up night.
As the first fireworks ignite over English Bay,
reflect in the windows of a highrise blocks away,
we wonder who's on the barge tonight,
if Jimmy Pattison is out on his yacht
with rich men and beautiful women,
dancing and drinking champagne,
if they lead better lives
than ours, and what we'd have to do
to get on board. You bring another beer
for your lover, fingers touching and eyes gleaming
in a flash so black and hot I wonder
how your husband does not see,
how he can know the names
of all the bands on the Eighties soundtrack
and not know he is losing his wife.
"Missing You" blares on the radio
as strangers clap and cheer

at the cookie-cutter heart traced for an instant
in the sky, then the weeping willows
weeping into the water.

CENTURY GRILL

We sat at a windy table
outside the restaurant,
the brick buildings scarlet
against the slate sky.
Cars passed in a metal stream.
I barely blinked, my lids rising
and slowly falling, reluctant
to lose anything to a fraction's darkness —
the sun and shadow across your face,
the waitress placing dish after dish
on the table with her long arms,
our reflections slipping
in the restaurant window.
The wind on my lips
tasted like lime.
You took off your wedding ring,
held it above the table
and let it fall,
a twist of gold that spun down
in the breeze, metal-hot
from the heat of your life,
and I reached out to catch it
· like the bridal bouquet.

It lay still and stony

in the centre of my palm,

blazing in the blinding light.

CHRIST CHURCH CATHEDRAL

in your mourning dress
you take centre stage again
pear hips swathed in pitch
the narrow compass of your pointed feet
the flicker of your hair and the flinch
of your smile

your presence at last makes real
his absence
the perfumed pulse
the rod of steel
your wiry body composed
of heat and sorrow
a will to live on
that has burned you down to bone

this is the tightening circle
of grief
Christ on the cross
rows of petalled faces in the pews
blue light drifting with bodies
and saints in stained glass darkening

now I can barely see you
for his body between us
composed of carbon monoxide
only the bend of your lily neck
the bouquets of wilting roses
their blood shapes
my lap stained with pollen

across the church our eyes meet like arrows
even now we mean each other harm
even dead he stands between us
your husband
his suicide a brush fire that consumed
everything in its path
even water
and oxygen and other things we needed to live

PART FOUR

FAMILY DRAMA

FAMILY DRAMA

In the sand you stage the play.
I know this theatre, it's housed me
for thirty years in its one room.
Here is the father, silent as balsam,
the mother a twig
wearing a belt of thorns.
You take the tiny father and mother
in your hands, they are moved
to kisses and tears under your direction;
this is the play you would dedicate to me
if you could, the story of reconciliation
and never-too-late.
All summer long we come to this beach,
sit by this log, and you try to give me back
my life. The father so soft between your fingers,
you could shape him into anything
but steel, or backbone.
The mother so sharp she leaves a splinter
in your thumb.
You search the sand for a stand-in
for me, topple the father
and mother onto the stone child,
smother her with love
until she sinks under the moon surface

of the beach, its craters and blue shadows.

You think she won't dream

the trapped dream again.

Other times the child is the size of your fist,

she charges at the puppet parents

and knocks them clear

into a coming wave.

Anything is better than silence, you say,

better than never coming to terms —

but it's what we choose. The day of grief

or the life cased in cement. The life of it.

DAMAGES

It begins in the family home, the source
that is also the lack. The dark place,
the space I've embraced,
the figures of the father and mother
feeding another day to the fire.
Perhaps this time in the dream of childhood
the bleak wind that howls in the sky
will pass over to another town, another shore,
and the tidal wave will bury your brute father.
But tonight I dream the house is a wheel
with another wheel turning inside it,
the father sprawled on the floor
like a man struck down,
the mother in the kitchen,
her hands on fire.
In the silence I could not move or speak
until the figure of the doctor appeared,
and just as the wheels slipped
he turned a bolt between his fingers
and fixed the walls and roof in place.
This is the answer to your question,
this is my dream of rescue.
No knights or white horses, but the doctor who descends
before the tragedy like a god from his machine,
too late to prevent the injury.

THE FLOOD

It happened the first time
I followed you upstairs. The black wave that towers
over our dreams of childhood swept over us
in bed where you wore your dead father's ring,
an onyx star that flashed over my body
like an omen. The next day I woke terrified
the way I'd once woken as a child
in the afternoon to find the parents gone
and nothing in the house but water
and wreckage. Did I imagine this?
I had dreamt the doctor dream again.
This time I was furious, shaking his desk
like a piece of driftwood — how could he allow
such destruction — and when he reached out
a wave of rage poured out of my body
and slammed into him so that we both rocked,
locked in our familiar drama. I woke
sleep-drunk, tumbled and rolled
in blue sheets; this was yesterday and
twenty years ago. The same ruined room
with a leaking skylight, the same crying out
for the father.

BOULEVARD OF BROKEN DREAMS

Last night I held a handful
of the blue pills, their bitter dust
a blanket on my tongue. When I swallowed
and set down the glass, it cracked in two
and water ran across the table
onto the floor, the way blood
bursts from the hurt body.
Across the alley the figure of my neighbour
stood watching at his window,
a "Boulevard of Broken Dreams" poster
on the wall behind him. We had never met,
though we had witnessed the other's
every gesture of sloth or sorrow. In bed
I waited for sleep to slam down
on the dream-figures of the father and mother
like a lid or heavy earth. Earlier that evening
the father's face had come over your face
as it hovered above mine in the firelight,
his skin fit tight around your shoulders
like a shroud, swathed the warm pillar
of your body, until you were lost to me.
I could no longer feel your kisses
or the pulse in your wrist, only myself

shrinking to the size of a child
in your embrace, and even smaller,
until my fingers webbed and eyelids fused
in the darkness inside the mother.

LAUGHING IN MY SLEEP

Twice it happened — you rolled me over
out of the mangled landscape of my dreams,
shook my shoulder and demanded, *What?*
What's so funny? My eyes flew open
to your room with its white skylight
and shells strung at the midnight window,
to your face huge as a father's above me.
For I had been laughing in my sleep,
and even as I struggled to the surface
of full wake, this otherworldly laughter
still hacked its way out of me,
no girlish giggle or cheerful chortle
but weird laughter from the deep,
the bottom of the black ocean
where my family still swims in the wreckage,
where every night I murder my mother
and lose my father, over and over.
It was like no sound I ever made
during the day, it was the laughter
of *an evil child*, you said later —
coming even after I clamped my hand
over my traitor's mouth, and you lay next to me
astonished, like a man who takes a step to the side
and finds he's suddenly standing in quicksand.

GROWNUPS

You were jealous of my colour dreams,
claimed to see only black and white
at night, so I closed my eyes
and invited you in.
Now we both live in the burning house
of childhood, miniatures of our parents,
doll husband and wife. Every night you bathe
in the lavender bathroom,
eat in the orange kitchen,
stand on the sundeck above a lawn of flame.
Tonight there is no cooking or cleaning to be done,
no work in the recessed world.
You sit idle in shirtsleeves,
I tug away the apron.
With nothing to do we punish
each other for entertainment,
one cold, the other colder,
a sequel to our daytime drama.
You might have gone your whole life
without finding me, the mirror self
you call the one, but we were lucky.
Now this house is your home too.

FORCED KNOWLEDGE

For Borislav Herak, captured Serbian soldier, awaiting interrogation for the murders of at least 29 Muslims

It's the pleading one you remember,
not the stoics who slipped silently into death,
the ones who gave their voices away even before
you yanked the blade across their throats,
their grainy animal flesh. Killing them the way
you now demonstrate for the papers, your elbow
sticking out awkwardly as an adolescent's,
making this gesture you first practised on pigs
on a grassy plot outside Vogosca.

Only twenty-one, your face angles out
from the newspaper photograph in luminous lines
as if thrusting through from another dimension,
breaking free of the background of guard and wall,
myopic reporter, window laced with wire.
The days leading to your possible execution
streak past like gunfire, but the nightmares remain suspended
near the ceiling of your cell, the man pleading for his life
and the life of his children. Why did he have to open his mouth
instead of sinking into the smile of that second mouth,
sinking back into himself, his red, clarion depths?
You toss, you turn, but always those eyes,
that mouth opening and closing

and then the bright flare of blood arcing through the air.
Pig's blood, you try to tell yourself,
but pigs make different sounds, no words.

Now the world press is at your father's doorstep,
to hear him say he wishes it had been him
instead of the anonymous men, women, children
kneeling on the floor so hard they bruised their knees,
leaning into sensation and life. As if
he could have been enough, as if with his throat
he could have spared the throats of others,
his familiar throat crosshatched with lines of sweat and grime,
that was salty and humid to a woman's tongue, sometime ago.
As if murder was something you had to get out of your system,
like a teenager's first, awful cigarette or case of beer.
But who knows if it would have been enough,
if the first deed would have led to abstinence or addiction?

Do you feel any remorse for what you've done?
That's all the reporters want to know, those are
the words you hear over and over — remorse, regret, a surge
of conscience leading to slashed wrists,
a noose spinning beneath a prison bulb.
You can't say you feel any of those things, though.

All you want to talk about is the dream.
That man, the one who asked to keep his life
in the terrible moment when his life suddenly
became a thing that could be taken away, when his life
hung loosely in the air like a wind sock,
like an idea that was up for grabs.

Why had he not stayed quiet, like the others?
It makes you shake your head, scratch your ear,
that he should keep coming back and asking for something
that is no longer yours to return. Too late,
you know you have the power to take something away
without the power to give it back. To say,
Here, go ahead, keep your life.
What do I want with you when my own father
is kneeling in that other corner, his shoulders bent back,
his throat offered up as though to receive a passionate kiss?

MIGRAINE

The aura is a rumour
of thunder in the distance,
building into a storm
that rattles the shutters
and the beads of the chandelier
before punching a hole
in the load-bearing wall.

The tap of construction
through the double-glazed windows
splinters your skull.
A forty-watt bulb blazes
like an eclipse on your retina.
The faintest trace of perfume
on your wrist and throat
is a field of a thousand flowers
pumping odour.

Pain floods the house,
the chambers of your mind,
the walls swell, the ceiling hiccups
and lifts like a lid on a pot boiling over.
You are tiny in its clasp,
as in grief.

The sun rises and sets, twice.
Finally the surrender
to drugged sleep, the sweet nothing
sleep of codeine.
In the absence of feeling,
an angels' chorus.

TRANSFERENCES

Eight years have worn pale
the paint in the green stairwell,
your doctor's credentials on the brass mailbox,
and if not for projection's transforming gaze
this building would seem a dollhouse
compared to the world it once was.
In the facing mirrors
I can barely see my selves
past or present in the underwater light,
yet as I climb the stairs to your office
the air thins, sight spirals inward,
and again I glance over my shoulder
for your shadow as you used to appear to me
some afternoons, walking silently behind me
until you were upon me and ahead.

The doors at the top of the stairs,
to the waiting room, the consulting office,
might each be a blank sheet scrawled with words
recorded yet not understood, a map given
but not a key. You remain at its centre,
my doctor, though I would not recognize you
passing on the street on a sunny afternoon
for all the faces I placed over your face.

Today we talk again of detachment
and disassociation, the hollow core
of the buried self, and this is the beginning
of words, the green heart of your office
the residence of poetry. This is the shape
my life has become, wider than the world we charted,
empty as the sphere I place again on your palm.

HEARTSICK

One afternoon walking on El Paseo
in hundred degree heat
we passed our reflections trapped that moment
and forever in an art gallery mirror titled
"Fairest of Them All."
But this winter has turned us to ice.
At night I slide my hands over my changed body,
its rock contours, its salt heart.
It is too heavy to haul from the bed
so I sleep all day, my mouth taped over
with a square of silver masking tape,
dreaming of helicopters crashing through windows
and mounds of dirt in my hands.

Yet in the doctor's office I shake
with the rage that boils beneath
the ice block, the frozen lake.
Such long years labouring here
and still I cannot see.
This is the maze with the stone centre,
the empty treasure inside the boxes
within boxes. The air is thick
like styrofoam, and the Oedipal pattern's tight weave

has me knit in its warp and weft,
its spiderweb fabric.
I am bundled snug in its sticky womb.

He says you were the father I murdered
by proxy, with your myopic tenderness
and weak body, your love for me I viewed
as if through the wrong end of a telescope,
a scrap in the face of furious hunger.
The doctor has stains on his pants
and his laces are untied.
His office is the palace I've longed
to live my life in, with ceilings too high
to touch, and a floor so cold it burns.
My marble home, my cramped quarters.
The stale afternoon air.

THE PSYCHIATRIST RETIRES

It's time, you say,
announcing this casual news
at the start of the session as though
it were a summer vacation or a conference
out of town, little cause for alarm
or affect of any kind. Somehow
you've turned sixty years old
in the space of a single conversation,
your toddling daughter now a teen,
your son sent off to university,
and at half your age I look around the office
and think, *But what will happen*
to the plants, who will take care
of them? You'd acquired so many
over the years that the room began to seem
like something out of a green dream,
soaked in chlorophyll, a tropical jungle
or a forest at night, all these plants
breathing, needing attention, their veins
pumping secrets to their buried hearts.
This was the only place I knew you.
As if you had no other life.
As if you lived in this office like a troll
under a bridge, a hermit in the hermitage,

suspended in formaldehyde light
until I blinked you into being.
All those years climbing the green stairs
to the sound of your coughing
behind the closed door, then the hour
of learning to listen to the meaning
behind the words, learning to listen to that voice.
We were removed from the world, but in it.
Maybe in the heart of it, in the bone cage of it.
Where the heart opens, closes,
stretches like the skin of a drum
in its monster terror. Tell me again
that absence isn't equal to vanishing,
to never was. I've learned your language
after all, pulled your silver self
through my veins like water,
here in this greenhouse room
where next year an architect
or an accountant will take your place,
narrow head bent to the papered desk.

ARSON

Tonight the house that mocks me in my sleep
rocks in a bed of fire.
The mother is trapped in the basement,
a spider in the centre of the web,
burning to a black crisp.
The father sobs on the dark sundeck.
He is himself and at the same time,
every other man. I press my body against his
to plead for everything I need.
For weeks the landscape has been changing,
the light dying inside your office.
We are approaching the place I locked away,
the desert with its spring of sorrow,
the hollow glass heart in the core of the maze.
Doctor, I've grown afraid of noises in the night,
and the white silence of days,
and young couples on the street
pushing baby carriages
remind me of my own death.
Yesterday you gave me a hammer and nails
to destroy the wooden dresser from childhood
that appears in all my dreams, but in my hands
they changed into a match and gasoline,
and the entire house went up in flames.

ACKNOWLEDGEMENTS

Several of these poems first appeared, in slightly different form, in the following publications: *ARC, Chelsea, Columbia, Descant, Event, Geist, Grain, The Globe and Mail, The Malahat Review, The New Quarterly, Poetry Nation, Prism international, Rampike, Sheffield Thursday* and *The Vancouver Sun*.

I also wish to thank the BC Arts Council and the Woodcock Fund for their support.

Evelyn Lau has published three previous books of poetry. Her first collection, *You Are Not Who You Claim* (1990) won the Milton Acorn People's Poetry Prize; her second, *Oedipal Dreams* (1992), was shortlisted for the Governor-General's Award, making Lau the youngest person ever nominated for this prestigious prize (she was twenty-one). Lau is also renowned as a prose writer. Her first, autobiographical book, *Runaway: Diary of a Street Kid,* was published when she was eighteen to worldwide acclaim. Her searing and arresting fiction — *Fresh Girls and Other Stories, Choose Me,* and the novel *Other Women* — has been published to rave reviews, and rights to these books have been sold in the US and around the world.

Now in her early thirties, Evelyn Lau is one of Canada's most remarkable young literary talents. She lives in Vancouver, British Columbia.